HORSEPOWER

ATVS

BY MANDY R. MARX

CAPSTONE PRESS
a capstone imprint

Blazers Books are published by Capstone Press,
1710 Roe Crest Drive, North Mankato, Minnesota 56003
www.mycapstone.com

Library of Congress Cataloging-in-Publication Data
Library of Congress Cataloging-in-Publication data is available
on the Library of Congress website.
ISBN 978-1-5435-2467-3 (library binding)
ISBN 978-1-5435-2475-8 (paperback)
ISBN 978-1-5435-2483-3 (eBook PDF)

Summary: This text discusses ATVs and their unique features.

Editorial Credits
Hank Musolf and Jessica Server, editors; Kyle Grenz, designer; Jo Miller,
media researcher; Kris Wilfahrt, production specialist

Printed in the United States.
PA017

TABLE OF
CONTENTS

The Ultimate Challenge.......... 4

Ready for Anything............... 10

Racing ATVs 16

Riding Safely 24

ATV Diagram 22
Glossary 30
Read More 31
Internet Sites.................... 31
Index 32

CHAPTER 1

THE ULTIMATE CHALLENGE

ATVs roar over bumps and through the air. The Baja 1000 is an exciting **relay race** for off-road racers.

relay race—a team race in which the members of the team take turns racing

The Baja 1000 began in 1967. Today, ATVs, **dune buggies**, motorcycles, and pickup trucks still race it—more than 50 years later!

Racers face nearly 1,000 miles (1,610 kilometers) of desert. Fans line the raceway. They watch the teams blaze through California's sand and heat.

dune buggy—a motor vehicle with large tires for driving through sand

The winning team gets a cash prize. But the real reward is the pride gained by completing this challenging race.

CHAPTER 2

READY FOR ANYTHING

ATV stands for all-**terrain** vehicle. These machines are small but strong. ATVs tackle even the toughest trails.

terrain—ground or land

ATV tires are made for rough riding. Big rubber **treads** help the tires grip any surface, from deep mud to loose gravel.

tread—a ridge on a tire that makes contact with the road

Riders can change their ATV tires for different surfaces. Tires with thick treads are used on trails.

TREADED TIRE

ATVs were designed for having fun. But farmers, ranchers, and rescue workers use ATVs for work. ATVs can go where other vehicles can't.

FAST FACT

ATVs can also help mow lawns, plow fields and snow, and haul logs and equipment.

CHAPTER 3

RACING ATVS

Racing ATVs is fun and exciting. Racers speed head-to-head toward the finish line.

Races are held on many types of courses. They range from dirt tracks to cross-country trails. Some races are even held indoors.

People of all ages race ATVs. Men, women, and children compete. Kids as young as 6 ride small machines.

HANDLE BARS

SHOCK ABSORBER

ATV DIAGRAM

TREADED TIRE

CHAPTER 4

RIDING SAFELY

State laws keep ATV riders safe. New riders can receive free training from the ATV Safety Institute.

ATV Safety Institute Training Course

FAST FACT
>>>>>>>>>>

Three-wheeled ATVs
were outlawed in 1988.
They rolled too easily.

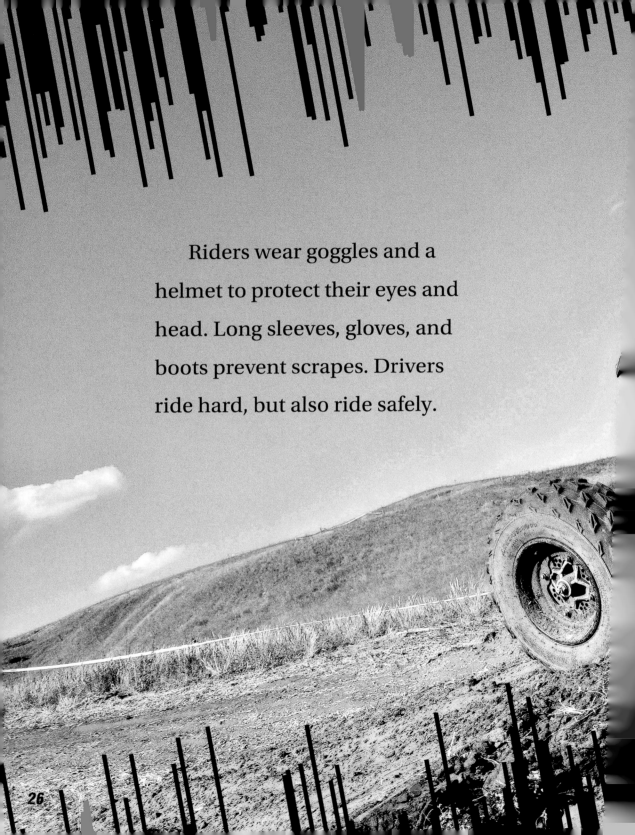

Riders wear goggles and a helmet to protect their eyes and head. Long sleeves, gloves, and boots prevent scrapes. Drivers ride hard, but also ride safely.

AT HOME IN THE MUD

GLOSSARY

dune buggy (DOON BUHG-ee)— a motor vehicle with large tires for driving through sand

goggles (GOG-uhlz)—special glasses worn by motocross riders to protect their eyes

relay race (REE-lay RAYSS)—a team race in which the members of the team take turns racing

terrain (tuh-RAYN)—ground or land

tread (TRED)—a ridge on a tire that makes contact with the road

READ MORE

Abdo, Kenny. *ATVs.* Off Road Vehicles. Minneapolis: Abdo Zoom, 2018.

Abdo, Kenny. *Dune Buggies.* Off Road Vehicles. Minneapolis : Abdo Zoom, 2018.

Scheff, Matt. *ATVs. Speed Machines.* Minneapolis: Abdo Pub., 2015.

INTERNET SITES

Use FactHound to find Internet sites related to this book:

Visit *www.facthound.com*

Just type in 9781543524673 and go.

 **Super-cool stuff!** Check out projects, games and lots more at **www.capstonekids.com**

INDEX

Baja 1000, 4, 7, 8

dune buggies, 7

fans, 7
farmers, 14

goggles, 26

helmets, 26

motorcycles, 7

racing, 4, 7, 8, 16, 18, 21
ranchers, 14
rescue workers, 14

safety, 24, 25, 26

tires, 7, 12, 13
trucks, 7